"Each poem in Deborah Gerrish's ⸺ that lifts reader as well as writer. Ge⸺ the human world is held in a heart f⸺ a feast of gorgeous, unexpected descriptions. 'Beauty is the breath of stars,' the poet writes. She has breathed such beauty onto every page."

—DONNA BAIER STEIN,
author and founder of Tiferet Journal

"'Let every breath praise,' counsels Deborah in poems that explore the natural world, spirituality, and family relations with intimate intensity and musical elegance. She lifts the 'cover of bereavement' to learn resilience from scars and reverence from brokenness. *Indeed Jasmine* is a testament to faith sustained through ardent observation; horses, oaks, egrets, 'dust caked' beneath fingernails, and the baba ganoush of the old country become 'the weight / of wet ink on the page,' a luminous stay against 'mortality's freight.'"

—MIHAELA MOSCALIUC,
author of Cemetery Ink

"*Indeed Jasmine* offers wonderful imaginative leaps and narrative surprises—'Pure Mathematics' features Einstein and turns out to be about a cat that watches *The Voice*, and 'Summer Fly' stars just that, before rising to an entirely different place. The collection shines with metaphysical contemplation and pungent evocations of place, both of them buoyed by generous portions of music, humor, grief, and hope."

—ELLEN DORÉ WATSON,
author of Pray Me Stay Eager

"Gerrish beautifully brings together different forms of poetry to express words that typically remain deep inside a person. Her poems draw out the vast array of human emotions in a manner that leaves the reader with a more profound sense of both his or her inner reflections and outer relationships. I invite you to engage these poems as a way to stir up your spirit."

—JEFFREY LEE,
senior pastor, New Providence Presbyterian Church

Indeed Jasmine

For Donna!

Indeed Jasmine

Whatever is, whatever was —
Whatever shall be known —
Is best expressed in the splendor
of a poem ⟶ Great seeing
you in person!
♡
Deborah

DEBORAH GERRISH

Deborah Gerrish
3/18/23

RESOURCE *Publications* · Eugene, Oregon

INDEED JASMINE

Resource Publications
An Imprint of Wipf and Stock Publishers
199 W. 8th Ave., Suite 3
Eugene, OR 97401

www.wipfandstock.com

PAPERBACK ISBN: 978-1-6667-4277-0
HARDCOVER ISBN: 978-1-6667-4278-7
EBOOK ISBN: 978-1-6667-4279-4

JUNE 16, 2022 3:43 PM

For JPG

The work of wings was always freedom,
fastening one heart to every falling thing.

—Li-Young-Lee

CONTENTS

THREE

FOUR

ONE

TREASURES

Staring west, a cotillion of Royal Terns
display black up-dos and orange beaks,
oblivious to my presence even when I
keer keer in their direction. Like a thief
I stuff my bag with moon shells, conch,
and sun-dried starfish—and tip-toe away.
The beach belongs to them. The sky belongs
to them. They allow me my treasures.

WINDTHROW

Chill winter air and it's only October.
Wings of dead leaves rustle, wrinkle,
fireplace smoke slaps the cold, hundreds
of acorns pucker our front yard.

I've had enough of sadness. A neighborhood
dog seizes, after swimming in green algae.
There's a rash of hurricanes, uprooted
trees, earthquakes all kinds of colossal loss.

On my way to the hospital, a naked man stops
traffic on Harlem River Drive. It's mother's third
visit. I melt into her room: rough sheets, lumpy
pillows, mechanized bed, untouched tray of tea,

oatmeal, peaches. Stale air. I arrange sunflowers,
Place them beside the bed pan. I study every fold
of her face, her even teeth, mouth curved upward
in the corners. I read to her. Blot her coughed up

blood with gauze. Semi-conscious. She rattles
as she breathes. I flip pages of the burgundy
devotional, her arthritic hand covers mine. We two.
In the smell of death, the smell of resurrection.

GOLDEN BELL

Don't be caught by the lemon chiffon
forsythia, genesis of spring,

with its branches shooting out,
spindly and young—

Kindly landlord of the red-bird
setting up housekeeping there.

Don't be caught by its yellowest yellow
luring monarchs, starlings, and bees.

This gold harbinger that tells us what we
already know: Beauty is the breath of stars.

SUMMER FLY

I trapped a fly into a plastic bag cinched
with a twist-tie. It relished shrimp tails

and tomato skins, dined on sweat,
the scraps of crusted bread. It soaked

in lemon juice, a cup of chai, coffee grounds,
cod bones, decomposed sweet potato fries,

and wandered slimy the terrain
of cucumber skins and watermelon rind.

I trapped a fly into a plastic bag cinched
with a twist-tie. It swam in white wine,

slurped on bits of bacon bits. It climbed
into a cradle shell of yellow yolk and turmeric,

its wings pinned by asparagus spears.
Three days later—sans eyes, sans air.

One day I'll lie beside the fly, close my eyes,
pass through the gate, the kingdom of song—

PURE MATHEMATICS

I have no special talent, I am only passionately curious.
—ALBERT EINSTEIN

And so love goes—
I heard him crying, one cat minus
one testicle, a new equation. He wore
a fentanyl patch, a cone collar

for two weeks, took cover in his safe
igloo bed. I had searched animal shelters
and found Isaac, defined laughter,
new feline cub, kitty cuddler.

Lustrous gold eyes, gray
and white tuxedo coat, pink
nose, pink gloves and shoes. Tail
dipped in charcoal with a white stripe.

Now he zooms from room to room,
travels the speed of light.
And so love goes—
Isaac is a feline poetry machine,

complete with his gravitational pull,
pure mathematics! Like Einstein,
he figures everything out. A wild
thing itching to sing, he watches

The Voice—but *National Geographic*
is his favorite channel. He observes
Alaskan wolves, shows no fear.
He's totally dependable—

follows directions, crouches and springs,
pounces after the stars.

CALAMITY

Faith travels from Trader Joe's to Costco
     to Stop & Shop, to Walgreens and Kings,
or to CVS from Shop Rite in search—

of toilet tissue paper. Coronavirus
     inconveniences in the valley of shadows.
          But what do I know. Over one hundred
years ago, survivors cobbled truths from death
marches across Anatolia.

And during her escape from
     the Armenian Genocide of 1915,

my grandmother was lucky
     to find a scrap of newspaper—
headlines swinging like a rope over
the bloodied Tigris.

WHERE THE SOUL SPEAKS OUT IN CONSERVATION

We face each other in the hallway mirror.
I raise a brow, my soul raises a brow. When

my eyelids flicker, she flickers hers, a visual rhyme.
Then a revolving door—thunderlight visits

in early morning hours. I brew green tea,
serve her buttered scones. She in her silkiest caftan,

bare feet. I in my blue robe, crocheted slippers. She's
curious about integrity. Asks am I comfortable in such

an uncomfortable world? Wonders can I trust her as ice-wind
bangs the kitchen shutters. We hush and nod to each other.

What do you know of sorrow, I ask? She tells me her grief.
Nine-inch iron spikes pounded through his hands and feet.

Her patience puddles like winter inviting spring's return;
she brushes off clinging chaff. Our thoughts lock.

Always her silver voice, a nightingale, quickens and vanishes.
Deep longs for deep in the radiant smoky glass.

A CALL FROM THE HINTERLAND

My friend visited her daughter's Kentucky
farm for a week, babysitting the little one,

while the couple completed Air Force exercises
in New Mexico. The sun drips like honey,

describes the cottonwood star, the rooster,
the fainting goats, albino peacock.

When she mentions Colonel, Jen's horse
since childhood—I listen closely. Gentle,

spirited creature gifted by a generous cousin—
chestnut eyes, braided mane. The prize beauty

traipsed the country with every relocation
during flight training. I listen even more closely:

all the time I imagine a hurry of stallions
flickering by, the color of nutmeg. Now at age

twenty, Colonel may have fatal pneumonia,
a costly risk to clear the lungs at $800 a day.

She recounts how a neighbor two farms over
came with his tractor this morning

to dig a grave by the side of the hangar,
how she wants to do well by doing good,

how she wishes to flee this round-about agony.
My breath shortens as she sobs over the phone,

whispers that Nathan the donkey
with the ancient eyes, cannot stop braying.

THE MAPLE TREE

Squirrels fail to recover up to 74% of the nuts they bury.
—CITED FROM A STUDY DONE AT
THE UNIVERSITY OF RICHMOND

More than the scent of chimney smoke in the autumn air,
more than baked apples, their shriveled leather coats
drizzled in syrupy cinnamon, more than a breath of breeze,
the rich earth, the ripened fruit on the vine. More than
muscat grapes, pumpkins, pomegranates— seeds and juices
bursting. When overworked summer is put to rest,
and gold-amber leaves are spent, I notice the squirrel
laboring in my front yard. He collects acorns and buries
secrets. To get his attention, I sing "Blessed Assurance."
Tell him I'm his friend, that this is the second spring.
Unsteady as a dog in a hammock, he stares back with his
round charcoal peepers. I tell him, take another look.
Maybe you should write them down, carve your hiding
places in the bark of the old maple. More than that, I tell
him *the poem is smarter than the poet.*

DIPPED IN WINE

This my spare poem,
let every breath praise—

let us make supper together,
let us sing as we season bread,

dip words in wine together—
this my beloved poem.

PROVERB

Here in this plague of wilderness, on our long ago farm,
I keep myself from fading as I separate the whites

from grays, stare out the window at shadows.
Dullness then visions: Proverb the peacock

rattles his wire-mesh pen. His purple tail
radiates hyacinth blue, metallic blue, mountain

blue—bronze, jade, an ostentation of sapphire.
In this wilderness, a celestial book of colors.

I inhale iridescence as the peafowl struts
his royal parade in search of a lifetime mate.

Proud body back-grounded by his halo,
my imagination snaps like elastic bands—

images of the sea loom, a thousand glitter
fireflies, invite every access to beauty.

My mind stands still as I come back to life, thanks
to the dauntless bee, relaxed stars, the sighing pines.

All through the night, I calm myself, a grasshopper
in a field of giants, the brow unknits, the heart softens,

and every day a masterpiece; the flowering
cornflower blue, a warm fire, a boatload of poems.

Glory ignites the skylight of heaven as Proverb
waves his fan of a hundred eyes!

Inside a palette of sky-blue wanderings—
like the peacock, God follows me everywhere.

A SECRET CORRESPONDENCE

Deep in the woods steeped
in winter's wintriness—
I take a midnight walk,

hug the trees, brush snow
from their weary white branches.
In their hidden chambers, a flurry

of owls play like a drone bass.
At early dawn, the sky and earth,
will be covered in a drift of gold,

a reverie—like a Hayden symphony.
Tall oaks lean close as lovers—listen
for harmonic whispers, I could swear

I hear them sigh. I know these woods
like an old friend. In the icy wind,
the nearly frozen oaks gesture. While

the world sleeps, limbs wave, signing
their language—their heart-secrets
in the stiff morning air.

DINING ALFRESCO

Sun setting red like a ruby pitcher of Sangria. Sidewalk café.
Cigar-box centerpiece with daisies, linen tablecloth. Cuban

jazz moves like smoke across the table. Silhouette of an aristocratic
figure with a shadowy beast on a retractable leash. I recall

Roethke's, *Natural shapes blazing unnatural light.*
Spanish bean soup, shrimp tapas, paella. My circadian

rhythm screetches to a halt, burns the wheel of time.
Fine-boned master with purebred—near our table railing.

Flan covered in caramel, Cafe Cubano, drizzled cream-design.
Scottish Deer Hound, the one Sir Walter Scott called

"the most perfect creature of heaven." His owner, now
inches away opens his plastic bag with metallic scooper,

scrapes up the royal dung. Calls out to us,
"Sorry, chap." You and I clink Mojitos.

You pantomime throwing daggers of crusty bread—
I search my evening handbag for the Mont Blanc.

BREATHLESS

As I drive north on Gulf of Mexico,
a colony of white egrets
near a cluster of silver palms,

their many shuffling feet creating
commotion at the edge of the golf
course water hole.

Gold beaks, gold slippers, gold eyes—
as if the kiss of spirited places
is opening the door a crack.

So I pull over. Slink across wild Florida
grasses, bundle the injured white heron
in my arms. Stroke its long

feathers like a small harp, and run my
fingers against its curved neck. Oh,
gorgeous creature of light—

TWO

I ASK MY MOTHER HER FAVORITE COLOR

Everything about her was pink—her ruby
thinking rooted more deeply than optimism.

Even the dress we buried her in five
days after father died. Shell-pink

bordered in shiny sequins. The same
dress she wore to my wedding. Twenty

years later, her joie de vive wafts through
my rooms like a blaze of gardenias.

A PAIR OF PELICANS

Scrambled vines of wild bougainvillea
scatter their waxy flowers on the bicycle path,

everywhere flaming hedges erupt ruffled hibiscus,
the buzz of flowering wings, birds of paradise.

Why does the slick fish crow perched on the glossy
yellow hydrant lament—*Ut-oh, Ut-oh?*

Beyond the Caribbean-green gulf, two pelicans
carry secrets on their long migration—

like long marrieds called across the threshold
of blurred horizon, they turn and wheel,

they wing a royal glide into the fogbow
above the open book of sea—

EVERYTHING, EVERYWHERE

He says . . . I will be exalted in the earth.
—PSALM 46:10

When I view "The Woman in Gold"
at the Neue, when I catch sight

of the St. Lawrence Seaway
or the Gulf of Mexico, even

with its red tide and lifeless fish,
I hear it. The Psalm pulses my head

when I tour the Alhambra, stand
on Ireland's Cliffs of Moher,

wander the Whitney, I feel it. He's
with me in the heights of Machu Picchu,

the depths of Death Valley, when I
wander city streets. Neruda

knew, Whitman knew it: Listen. Be Still.
It echos, as I breathe the salt-sky and waves,

everywhere that silkaline silence
of greatness bundled in eternity.

ECLIPSE

Tommy Friedlander stalked me on the playground
every day at lunchtime at John Greenleaf Whittier
School. The sun with its corona gold would be lighting

up the sky, he'd begin his cosmic dance. Rebellious
looking boy chasing this starry-eyed sixth grade
classmate. Like a solar eclipse, his black cloak

flying with its crystal-shell button hooked about
his thin neck, he'd dart the field like a bat in daytime.
The mahogany cane, with his grandfather's initials

TJF, III, in the hands of this boy with lackluster
chestnut hair, cowlick, moon face—freckles scattered
above his brow, his leaden profile clad in darkness,

the cellophane bag of silver-wrapped candies
—chocolate kisses like diamonds he'd spill
at my feet, all over my white Keds.

WHAT'S IN A KISS?

Bonobos, most sexual of our fellow
apes, are fond of French kissing.

Hershey kiss, Eskimo kiss,
stolen kiss, the "mwah"

of the air kiss. The mother
bird regurgitating food into

her chick's mouth at feeding
time, kiss. Legend tells us

that somewhere on Mauritius
Island dodos even kissed.

The art of the art of kissing.
Ah!!! Even nature gets it—

WATER'S EDGE

Red tide, dead grouper—
orchid perfume on my wrist
rejoices the heart.

***

Waves turned inside-out—
torn umbrella on clay sand
washed in the mud storm.

***

A harvest moon sparks
the pointed-billed kingfisher
to spear a perch.

***

Slender flamingo—
lingers beside the pools
wading on one leg.

AN OLD INVENTION

Barnum and Bailey—like a reverie,—
the wild peace of childhood, the tranquilizer
of memory. Elephants, lions, the glittery

circus girls riding horses and camels. Clowns
in their fire-red wigs. Madison Square Garden,
a child's star-lit park beneath the Big Tent.

Trapeze artists swing from risky heights
like a tribe of lemurs. Tightrope wires, chords
of hope. Just last summer, I visited the museum

in Sarasota, sat in the weathered train car
Ringling and his wife Mabel toured the country in.
How they hauled their living freight, an entire

circus in the back railway-cars. At the Ringling
mansion, statues, fountains, lush grasses,
pineapple and royal palms—the bronze David,

the rows of Victorian roses. Ah—yesterday and
yesterday—the lost years of childhood, the old
invention of the circus. Its authors. At the dinner table,

mother would take us back to when the circus came
to Paterson. How the train would pull into the station,
with tigers and elephants thundering down saw-dusted planks,

two by two, followed by trunks of capes, crates of scarves
and trinkets, cages of rabbits and snakes,—
all steered down the ramp to a new world.

As I think back, all of it is gone and past. The lost years
of the circus; those unicorn years. But then my mind
wanders to non-tranquilizing thoughts of my adolescence.

Reminiscence. The original pinstripe vending machines.
A nickel apiece—Musketeers, Almond Joy, Chuckles
—tucked in a corner near the big top, adjacent to the

cigarette machine. I'd sneak back there with a few
coins, deposit five cents, and the manual lever delivered
what I wanted. Thirty-five cents a pack for Marlboros

unfiltered. Cool and reckless. Adolescence.
Wordsworth called it "dizzy rapture." But just today,
I think how my sweet tooth has changed.

Kind Bars and granola bars—twelve dollars
for a box of eight. Cheers to good health, smoking
is taboo. Internet-sophisticated replaces

the Greatest Show on Earth, a new century.
But I'm an ancient invention, wrapped in sinew,
muscle, bone, a made thing made from dust,

with eternity scratching at my soul. Still the same,
not the same. As mortality's freight hangs on
this frame, I wish for the wings of the circus lion.

UP IN THE AIR

our plane

    cuts through

a pergola

    of white candy-floss

coasts foothills

    of open sky

cloud-stepping

    white cumulus

their edges

    a bric-a-brac of gold

against sentimental

    blue

AFTER THE JUNIOR HIGH SADIE HAWKINS DANCE

Stealthily, to escape the chaperones up in the bleachers, Joey and I slip through the heavy gym doors onto the field to make out under the oak. I wear his ring with its sapphire crystal facets on a chain around my neck. We sputter and kiss like we're slurping chocolate egg crèmes through straws. What do we know? His leather jacket cushions us from the cold November ground. He takes a drag from his Marlboro and passes it to me. Inhales, exhales. Then back to the work of making out. We try to get comfortable on the frozen ground. Me in my green pleated jumper with white ruffled blouse. My camel hair coat flung across a low tree limb. Our bodies steaming, neighborhood cedar chimney-smoke arousing my senses. And meanwhile my father, idles his Olds Starfire in the parking lot, puffing his briar-wood pipe, waiting to pick me up.

BROKEN, BEAUTY

"Just passing through," he tells me. The poet of St. Armand's Circle sits day after day at a card table set on the sizzling Florida sidewalk. His sign reads, "Come fly with me," like the blue heron he has sketched on it. Ten dollars per poem. Pounding his 1950's Remington, he writes on demand about love and loss, loss and love. His full beard and missing front tooth, his visor of hope, his portable atelier near Hemingway's where he grabs a bean burger and sweet potato fries before launching into the next poem. I say to myself, *A person can't help but gain wisdom from all this eating and thinking and making art.*

The charmed 10 year-old with corn silk hair and lapis eyes requests a poem for her brother. She twirls her long braid as they go back and forth like sandpipers on the Gulf sand with questions and answers about her brother. Fragile as he waits in his wheel chair under the striped awning, his incantations are spiraling the royal palms. And the poet, whose service Lab naps on the pavement, uses his sleeve to wipe the sweat rushing like Niagara down his beard. He hits the keys and hammers out the lump in his throat. All I can do with this other-worldly scene is stare at one cracked vase of brilliant sunflowers.

SCARS

I collect scars the way I collect stones,
but hold them tight in raw fists,
cast them out

against the water. Memory
returns to deface and gnash
my soul in the night. Scars

from losses. Scars from scars.
Who's to say which stabbed
the deepest or the longest?

I tour them
as from a boat adrift —
coastline barely visible.

Scar from finding him
dead in his recliner, the 6:00 news
droning through rooms,

scar from mother passing away
in the hospital, just four months after
her daughter dwindled from cancer.

Like a gull plummeting
in currents above the bridge,
a young woman freefalling from losses—

The more you feel a place, the more
it calls you back. Scars—etched footsteps.
Signposts. Mirrors. Milestones.

A collaboration of tattoos. Once
inflamed, once scarlet fistulas. Tracks
of thick skin in gold-relief.

STATE-OF-MIND

Last night, from his porch, the young man watches
as a mother raccoon tugs at dead ivy splayed in its clay pot,

twines herself in tendrils of trailing leaves,
shrieking. The man's head pulses like a screech-owl.

The roof piled is bowed by frozen snow, gutters hemmed
with daggers —the sun lost in a marble sky, as the raccoon

paces the wreckage, circles the knocked-over stool, squeals.
Never taking a breath, she storms the street in the grey daylight.

Wind yodels through the man's skull as he retreats to his father's house—
bed unmade, keys, wallet, haphazard on the highboy. Shades drawn

silent as the room, a cloisonné vase swelling with amaryllis, motionless
on the windowsill. Coffee pot unplugged. Nostrils burning.

Through the garage window, sleet falls up, oaks slump down, clouds
exit the ground. On the kitchen wall, the clock skips widdershins.

GRIEF

No one ever told me that grief felt so like fear.
—C.S. Lewis, *A Grief Observed*

I knew there would be a dark tangle of trees—
velvet gloom, quickened beneath the sighing
sun forbidden entry, maybe a canopied den, but
who could anticipate a fanned web with clotted spider veins,
vast carnivorous trees, black widow, hourglass abdomen,
the macabre small tank of ink, eight-jointed legs spilling,
arched like a hideous door hinge, all hope lost for a lifting
of sorrow, any beam of light in the back-water of my mind?
A pitch dark pit awakes me. Would anyone ever raise
the rusted cover of bereavement with juvenile grunts—
steady across the floor of soil and fungus? All I see is a block
of obsidian, mirroring a deeper darkness there, an unexpected
tomb of discovery, unguarded, assailing. Pain, fierce and continuous,
like an amputated wing, wounds buried in its mud-soaked secret:
anger, a glint of light.

MIDSUMMER EVENING MEDITATION

The moon is a beauty mark on the face
of God, the stars are the freckles on his hands—

the sun, the lifeblood of his eye,
makes a way where there is no way,

and seabirds, weaving in and out
of clouds, idle in the sky

like his grace-filled thoughts toward
his daughters, toward his sons.

DREAMING THE GARDEN STATE

I imagine the landscape of Eagle Rock Reservation
overlooking the Hudson. New York City, the other side
of the river. Route 9 connecting ocean towns from Avon

to Cape May long before the secret got out. The crested
cardinal with his slurred whistles. New Jersey. Wild canary.
Blue meadow violets. Cranberry fields, blueberries,

tomatoes. Eggplant like the darkest wine in aubergine
wineskins. I call out Princeton. Paramus Blue Laws,
Monmouth thoroughbreds moving like the wind.

Rutherford, Paterson, magnolia and peonies. Hymns
that run through my veins. Nanna's summer tapestry
of meals, *children should be seen and not heard.*

I trace the wooden Cyclone rollercoaster of the Palisades,
Votee Park's ice-pond, flashes of skates, bonfires,
that first time feeling of driving my second-hand Chevy.

Murray the K's "Swinging Soiree" blasting on the radio.
I envision Atlantic City, conch shells, one-legged sandpipers,
Lucy the Elephant Hotel, the salty air of boardwalk.

Even as the world circles, I recall Jersey, my mother of pearl.
I claim this dream winged out to sea like a cormorant
on an enormous wave as the shoreline fades.

THREE

WONDERLAND

We visit Kiddie Wonderland every Saturday
in July. It's not exactly the level of the Palisades
with its Sky Ride, Giant Slide, Saltwater Pool,
or the infamous Cyclone. But what do we know?
This is our Araby. My sister wears a pleated sundress

with matching short cape fastened around her shoulders,
patterns of tiny red rosebuds. We launch from our house
arm and arm, skipping over cracks on the sidewalk,
turn down the block, pass a farm, the cascading ferris wheel
appears like a huge butterfly. She says, *the carousel music*

fills me like pitchers of iced-lemonade. I've slung my Brownie
camera over my shoulder, and carry a beaded purse with bills,
some pennies, and a buffalo nickel. I pay our 50 cents admission.
Today we choose the whip of spider tentacles. As the attendant
shuts us in, we squeeze into the cab like two grapes on the vine.

My sister's kangaroo pockets are stuffed with strawberry
Bonomo's Taffy, and we play tug-of-war and stretch
the chewy candy between us, stuff our mouths. Riding
the small train, we nibble caramel candied apples:
at the Penny Arcade, win three goldfish, buy two sticks

of pink cotton candy, imagining strands of angel's
hair. As usual, she pleads with me to ride the kiddie
roller coaster with her. I take photos of her acting
like a little screech owl with her head turning,
with her cape-wings horizontal. Click. Click.

Looking back at pictures of her in those mystic blue
plastic sunglasses, too large for her sweet-heart
face, I think, *Those were our Shirley Temple days.*
We ride Casper Boats in circles in the man-made
pool. I snap a shot of her glossy grin—

she unscrews the steering wheel, waves it in the air as
boys float by; sticks her tongue out at the camera.
Boys on bumper cars call out, then whistle.
One Day they will take us on the Flight to Mars, I say,
as she frees her balloon, lets it vanish through the clouds.

I WAKE AT SUNRISE

to savor the strawberry cream
of first light. Morning glories,

bearded irises, guardian-blue violets,
the emerald fields dotted with haystacks,

the fire-charged touch of blaze—
marvel of turquoise sky, sun-drenched dew.

Dawning masterpiece,
    woven candy floss—daybreak

WHAT I CAN'T EXPLAIN

This morning I search for my mother—
two dozen years since her passing,

I step inside the family house, breathe in
the roasting lamb, inhale fennel

in the seams of the drapes, coriander
like perfume in the woven Persian rugs.

I visit her kitchen, clanking kettles
and copper pans. Search the bedroom,

her scented closet, chiffon dresses,
wool sweaters. Scan her bookcase.

Open a book of poems she loved,
but she's not here. I step out

into the backyard and stand beneath
the resolute magnolia, her wide arms.

Tender petals scattered words of silver.
I wait. Listen—nuzzle there.

REGALIA

Moon cactus, nectar for bats, perfume
for butterflies, pollen for bees in their wax houses—

a slice of moon, wraps its afterglow around the stars,
lights its lamp-beams in many worlds. If I stop

to listen, I hear the spin of sighs. Voices of cicadas,
catydids—the yen of it all. What makes these echoes?

The voice of God, the thunder of his kettle drums,
and the cymbal-hush of the redbird's breath.

They call to me like a childhood friend,
the whole of nature like a cantata—calling

across the earth, across the ages, beneath the blue.
Listen. Here on this hiking path,

you and I hold hands and share the sad news.
Before long we're distracted: a young robin

bounces along, red breast zig-zagging, a worm
hanging from his beak—

ALL DAY LONG HEAVEN COMES TO MEET ME

First the garden-center worker whose nametag reads "Heaven"
    as I squint at the lettering,

then the toy poodle barking at the lamb displayed on the church
    lawn crèche scene.

Sanderlings chase waves back and forth, the littlest one bouncing
    on one foot;

egrets with gold sandals ramble, and splash, and chant,
    legs running twigs,

sewing machine needles stitching their hieroglyphics
    in the powdery sand.

Silver date palms dry their feathered tendrils in the breeze, chuckling
    like afternoon dowagers.

Yesterday their full-headed plumes blew each way in upheaval,
    wet leaves in a tropical storm, a leather raincoat.

My brow wrinkles to see that tiny bird hopping on one foot, the other
    one is missing,

tucked like a folding chair under his apron, or an amputee!
    I cry out to help him then realize he's a joker.

If you want to know about the soul, ask the Great Blue Heron with his
    folded neck as he skims

the gulf coast at sunset, or the fulsome moon as it torches a hiking path
    through the sea,

my heaven is here, by the sea—I was born to be lost in the deep,
    a starling on a studio boat.

DURING THE PANDEMIC

The Covid shutdown is like children
being sent to their collective rooms,
forever. It feels like an eternal snow day

that loses its buzz. But the church offers
a shelter-in-place Zoom Open House.
Its Red Sea—is the browser window.

FAITH IS

the murmuration of starlings, shifting shapes,
    pulsing twilight, a banner waving

inside the chest—the scarlet flash of tanager
    across a car windshield at dusk,

the mechanical synthesis of bluebird's
    perfect-woven nest. Faith is

the lit canopy of greenest leaves against
    stained-blue spaces, a cathedral window.

It's inside this poem—the weight
    of wet ink on the page.

But let the expression on faith's face
    be an open secret like the pansy's

gold calligraphy. Let it be the thing
    with roots, the thing with wings—

the road to Golgotha, *The Man of Sorrows,*
    his thorny crown, his bloodied stripes,

the words "Father, forgive them,"
    the dazzlingly empty tomb.

EARLY MORNING FLIGHT

Crystalline blue out the window,
life vests under our seats, "Ya-ya-ya,"

sings a talced baby behind us.
The caged terrier's bark sounding like

Latin, with the New York City skyline
to the left, a flight attendant on the intercom

drills the emergency exit plan, iPads, iPhones,
computers jam the skies. I unfold the newspaper,

announce a headline to you: "Necco Wafers,
Taste of Childhood and Chalk, Near the Final Crunch."

Flavors like a "tropical drywall," a "plaster surprise," prod
me to defend my candy icon, which predates the Civil War.

We share a Kind Bar, a glass of red wine. My
head rests on your shoulder. Clouds thin as breath,

my beloved and I, locked in a ship of metal, soar
through rococo configurations of peonies, hedges

of primroses, a waft of sweet alyssum.
I think, nature fashioned from nature—

tunnels of stars, the dragon sun,
the crescent sea, and all of humanity.

Frost was wrong. Something gold can stay.

ANOTHER SPRING

Patches of tar bubbles popped along the curb
like summer simmered in dormant desire,

mid-June sweaty young bodies, neighborhood boys
running bases like fireflies, lanterns flashing,

June blurred into fiery August beneath willows that lined
our block, we breathed fresh air, the humid thrill

of being cut loose, boys tagging each other,
dirt-stained T-shirts, the whiff of becoming men.

I pitched and batted in khaki shorts, madras blouse, braids
with ribbons streaming behind, ate Neccos, chewed

Wrigley's gum until I heard my name echo from the top
of the hill as mother waved me home for dinner.

My trophies were scratches from mosquito bites, prickly branches,
as I launched into womanhood. One day we stopped coming

out of our houses to do what kids do, emerged bright-new
into another spring like a tripped switch—

Not yet knowing how the dusky light unspools into a peony
the shape of love.

TURTLE BEACH

Next to the frayed cabana chair wedged deep
in the powdery sand—seltzer, sunscreen,
tote with a cache of books, pairs of flip-flops
and sandals like four flippers. I am at home.
From behind fishermen, I peer through
binoculars at pelagic birds, sight an albino
pelican with a small snapper flapping in his beak
like a rubber toy. The portable radio forecasts
"Here Comes the Sun"—I hold my breath.

Breakers wrestle the shoreline, tag-chase gulls,
churn tinted scalloped shells underfoot. A towel
covered in gold pineapples enfolds me. Windblown
sand all through that afternoon into dusk until a sun
shower sky opens to bright headlights. A clutch of teenage
sisters emerge from the dunes, just as a group of green
sea turtles fend a restless path toward the white waves.
A blonde-haired lifeguard swaggers toward the girls,
swoops in to charm the brood of hatchlings before moonlight.

OCEAN JAZZ

syncopated

consecutive

drum rolls

followed

by sweeps

of drum brushes

fading along beside

one thousand chimes

of water-color

jade against

cymbals

clashing

swept strokes

on the beach

held loose

TENNIS PLAYER'S LAMENT

I miss the clay courts. Thick red dirt.
    Terra cotta stains on my skirt ball-pockets.
        Canvas tennis shoes clumped

with dirt. I miss the all white palette of wooly socks,
    regulation Bermuda shorts, cable-knit sweaters,
        collared shirts & crocodile logo.

Woven with cow-gut, I miss my wooden Dunlop,
    triangular frame, screws tight against warping.
        Wilson tin cans lined on shelves in Cowan's

Athletic store on Main. Just yesterday, I breathed
    the freshly opened can of tennis. I yearn to hear
        pinging back and forth across the net.

I miss those vanishing
    summers strung together like
        an endless game,

I miss the overheads, backhands,
    and drop shots, Fila dress & racquet,
        a buckler and sword.

Alone in my room, I long for
    my poachable moments. My losses
        buried back there.

Still in communion with the art of tennis—I
    imagine a stylized dance of love. Matisse
        understood the tumbles, stops and starts,

the springing, the flourishes. Celebration of sky, earth,
and body, wheeling and twisting—I miss
the elements in unity, the dust caked

beneath my fingernails,
red clay in the creases
of my fingers.

THE WHOLE EARTH IS LIKE A POEM

The fulsome moon, the dancing bay, the circling
glitter-light. Sculpted mountains, clouds above
the glassy sea, the cinnabar sunset. The call
of the shofar, an ostentation of peacocks, cedar trees
sproutings from bird droppings. Sparks of fireflies,
scattered stars. Wildflower. Apple blossom. Azalea
ablaze. Dramatic forsythia. Bluebell constancy.
Birdweed, Birch, Bird's foot. Courage of poplars,
humility of cherry trees. Indeed lilac. Indeed jasmine.
Delight, delighted, endeared by me. Artist's claim, artist's
voice. Blush. Captivation. Perfumed petunias. Snowdrops
of hope. Light-hearted shamrock. Rose, Austrian. Lovely.
Adoration, reverence, afterglow. A burning bush.

LIBRARY VISITOR

For Charles Simic

Yesterday a visitor left a book behind
on the pine table: *The Encyclopedia of Angels*

covered with dust, flakes of cracked leather.
It was the first day of spring. I felt the urge to write

about angels, the host of pure wings, but
I became achy-eyed—

sun glaring off my MacBook Pro. When I opened
the volume, no angels flew out. No messengers

with shimmering curls, no robes draping silk pages,
no rouge-red cheeks, no eyes afire with gold-leaf light.

Half awake, I sipped a Poland Spring and like a seam
opening up in the day, I heard the deafening cacophony

of a waterfall. Leaves flung open like a sacred
manuscript, first a flutter, then a thunder. And there

he towered, and I, *a little lesser than the angels*—
I with my tortoiseshell glasses, floral blouse,

chiffon skirt. My fountain pen on the wooden desk.
I looked up, dark sliced by a blade of light.

Glory too great to be trapped in a book, I thought.
He tossed me what resembled a pen, traced the gilded air.

FOUR

MY GREAT MISTAKE

is to not continue my mother's creative project—

her wallpapered rooms crowded with shooting stars,
hallways covered with burnished glass reflecting

light. And the hi-fi blasting Mozart throughout the house
like haunting laughter from sisters in the backyard.

Such a mistake not to continue my mother's creative design.
The French portrait of roses above the fireplace,

the vase of gardenias on the mahogany Steinway—her paints
and sable brushes, her tonic of color rising from the cellar.

I often dream what it would be like to tie pink ribbons around
my ankles and dance across the blue earth into eternity,

and dance the blue earth into eternity.

BUTTERFLY TANGO

Butterfly, butterfly, rest on me—
take me for a primrose mistake me for a tree.

The sea's distant voice is calm, the forest
a psalm. Between whispers, shaded lilacs

sway. Butterfly, butterfly, bringer of light,
on loan from the throne room in royal flight,

your orange-tipped wings a lacework pair—
How do you dance through the daisy-ed air?

Butterfly, oh butterfly, forget-me-not please,
I'm here beneath the dogwood waiting patiently.

Bless me, with your presence,
winged kaleidoscope of touch,

sparkle my heart wildly— Show up!

Show up!

CHARMS

strung on a fine mesh chain—
    petite scrolled heart with a ruby chip,
gold cross, 18 karat filigree.
    Her first tiny solitaire diamond,
the miniature Star of David embossed with
    round sapphires—

These hang about her neck as the sea glitters.
    Delivered from the desert,
her hard journey.

AT THE TENEMENT MUSEUM

I'm thinking of my father. Families boxed
in chicken coops, thirty apartments blurred
into one building, late 19th century tenants,

turn of the century dreams. Winding flights
of staircase, their only outhouse at the city curb.
Narrow shot-gun apartments—no windows.

The Irish couple's American-born infant
screams in a tin bucket-cradle beside them.
A line's strung above basin, scrub board,

and stove. Laundry limp over two sisters's bed.
The living room, a dorm by night, a workshop
by day. Four sons sleep on the couch, feet

elevated on crates. At daybreak, the family bends
to their work, cutting, designing, fitting, and sewing
dress patterns for Sears on their Good Housekeeping

sewing machine. *A better life than in Ireland
on the farm?* In summer, heaps of horse manure
steam in the streets. In winter, a dead horse

—they carved him up once he thawed. This
afternoon, I empty the ashtray. I scan the city
from the window of the Algonquin. I'm thinking

of my father as a young boy living on 9th Avenue
in 1918, his father dying of the Spanish Flu.
A family of ten stuffed into a one-room

apartment, his mother's sister Suzy— a teenager
in a thin dress. Her infected leg. They wrapped it
in newspaper and garlic. She died from gangrene.

THE STAND OF TREES

How they praise the maker
    in their ancient sanctuaries,

branches raised like worshippers,
    they sing hymns to the forest.

Consider the grove of dancing aspens
    beneath a threatening sky,

the panache of paper birches, dressed in silk-white
    bark and dazzling leaves, the most

stylish outfit I've seen on a tree. Or consider the drama
    of the banyan, drenched in braided ropes

swaying like a curtain of armor.
    I've never heard a tree moan and suffer

from wanderlust, never knew a root-gulag
    to travel far unless thirst demanded it.

Never observed skirmishes between oaks
    and elms though they too have clay feet.

They trade our carbon dioxide for their oxygen,
    the lifeblood of humanity, a constant kindness.

They signal family trees when predators eat their leaves,
    they're not frivolous, not covetous, nor afraid

of the future, but relentless like waves. They are their own
    timeless offspring— bending in the green air.

CONSUMPTION AS ART

Fashion fades, only style remains the same.
—Coco Chanel

Heaped on her mid century
    modern loveseat—

      leopard
pants with zippered-pockets
gray lace & denim skirt
    white sleeveless tee
        black leggings
black silk blouse
      pleated dress with torn bric-a-brac hem
    blistered matelasse jacket
red tattersall
    vest with missing buttons
brushed
velvet headband—a jumbled pyramid

a leaning tower—
tossed striped-stained scarf
jacquard Aztec sweater
paisley mismatched socks
navy leather
belt
    faux fur
cross-body bag
blue brocade heels
 flip
 flops

—an assemblage
of conspicuous consumption
stockpiled in
    her California closet.

LIKE KOI IN DEEP WATER

That first kiss—not
sweeping from one side
of the face to the other,

not a butterfly kiss, air kiss,
chocolate kiss. More than
a spin the bottle bashful kiss.

His worn leather jacket
rolled into a pillow. His
soft hands, wide blue eyes.

Her speckled sea-green
pleated jumper, ruffled
blouse, pearl buttons.

The heavy scent of damp
trees, the oxygen-rich air.
Two teens vowing forever.

His nicotine breath, the school
ring swinging like a fishing line
on a chain about her neck.

More like eager lips. Clumsy
tongues skim lips' edges—
smacking, sputtering, splashing.

Gulping, slurping, sucking
stolen breaths of upstream-
freedom as the silver moon

turns its light switch on
and off. Something more like
cold-water kissing turns its

light switch on and off.
Something colder like
a slap in the face—

more like a swim in a lake.

ODE TO LIGHT

Every morning brings some light.
  A crack of blue, a candle in the gray,
    a coat of heaven's colors.

Glossy honey in the swollen hive
  radiating orange blossom-scent,
    mountain laurel and goldenrod,

wildflowers swathed in polished amber,
  layers of water-music blazing
    and the brilliant skirl of bagpipes.

The blond dragon sun, though he could be
  kicking his heels, follows the rules every
    morning at sunup, every evening

when he drops below the horizon to another
  world. And what about the steady rain?
    With its drama—on again and off

throughout the seasons—faithfully soaks roots,
  fattens weeds, encourages
    the peony to bloom.

Skies show off their spangled stars
  and heavenly bodies, and all of nature
    dazzles the world.

The raised branches of birches and maples flash
  their limbs like banners. Sparrows and thrushes
    sing praises. Wings, and voices, voices

and wings. Praises to the Dayspring—even Einstein, looked
  beyond his telescope and notebooks, and thought—
    What if I could ride a beam of light across the universe?

THE PETITS FOURS

White pelican
fishes from the dock,
one eye closed.

On the glass stovetop—
black & white checkered teapot
offers a visual rhyme.

Sunflowers multiply
seeping outside lines—
in the coloring book.

The strawberry breeze—
frozen summer popsicle
tickles the tongue.

THE MAIN THING

Fresh light in the shadow of dusk
another spring better than the last

pure words distilled three times
no, seven times over

church cat yowling from the bell tower
sea-waves that glitter like lightening bugs

porch swing empty in moonlight
warrior grasshopper in a nest of crows

blithesome willow in the linen breeze
the ascending notes of the harp

signposts as stars in a night sky
God's fingerprints everywhere

IN THE WORLD OF LOSING HIMSELF

For Yehuda Amichai

Here he sits at his writing table with paper
and pen. Computer shoved to the side,

the Psalm etched on the walls
of his mind. Recites it three times a day.

He scribbles his agonies, ink running
the pages like a marathoner.

HER FAVORITE FLOWER

Twitterpated wings
    a breeze streaming through

the delicate faces of pansies
    wrapped in linen

Each fragrance sealed
    like children's given names

No wonder
    my mother loves pansies

You can tell by the way she
    pats their feverish heads

sprays their dusty faces
    as they tag-chase the wind

By the way she strokes their necks,
    shades, feeds, and snips them gently

You can tell by the way
    she falls at their feet

BABA GANOUSH

I learned the word *eggplant* when I was just three—
its curved form, compact like our cat's hourglass shape.
Some the size of hen's eggs, some oblong like cucumbers.
Glossy purple. Deeper than magenta. The color of dark

petunia. Every July fourth, our father would select
a dozen light-weight eggplant from the garden.
Place them in a tin after rinsing, then juggle them for us
like precious amethysts, majestic in sunlight.

We never dreamed he would drop one! Outside
our screened-in-porch, he'd prepare the barbecue-grill
purchased across the river at Rickles, sprinkle
lighter fluid, and fire up the coals.

He'd place the eggplant—92% water—
on the grate to roast in their purple jackets,
their sleek aubergine, elongated skin, charring.
He'd turn them slowly, what seemed like hours

—pierced them with a fork as a doctor giving an injection
for the patient's own good. He'd peel back burnt layers
as stems fell into the fire and the eggplant shriveled
to half their weight, allowing smoky-steam to escape,

awakening our nostrils like eucalyptus. We kids lined single-file
in the backyard with our starry paper plates. Waved small
American flags, watched him fill the ceramic bowl, mash
the golden pulp with lemon, garlic cloves, and tahini. Finally,

he'd fold the Baba Ganoush into the warm home-made pita bread
that mother delivered on a tray. Sing and dance the room
with me again, Old Country— a salute to oriental rugs,
orchards, and watermelon fields.

ALAKAZAM—

out of the boneyard,
out of dusty ruins
out of what Yeats calls
a mouthful of air

—you wrestle, as I am doing now,
    like Jacob with the Angel.
Poems may be born twice,

first in the imagination, then
    in a calligraphy of sound.
Once in the head,

then twice from the heart.
    And the child-poem, that new birth,
uproots whatever you thought possible—

TALKING TO GOD

You are the Gardener, the Governor,
the Architect. I am a blue glass roof

that shatters at the slightest,
a red bird storm-swept

in a scrap of nest. You
are the magnolia, the entire

poem. And I? The em dash—

the unspoken heart-skip,
the unfinished line

Acknowledgments

M Y DEEPEST APPRECIATION and gratitude to Sean Nevin, Ellen Dore Watson, Maria Mazziotti Gillan, Laura Boss, Diane Lockward, and Sondra Gash, for their encouragement and poetic wisdom, and for the larger community of poets where I have found a place for guidance, and for the support of my family, and special applause to Isaac, another inspiration. Finally, thank you to my husband, Jim, who supports and encourages all of my writing endeavors—with love and patience.

Thank you to the editors of the following publications. Some of these poems have appeared in the following journals, some in earlier versions or with different titles:

Adanna: "Consumption as Art," "Eclipse," "I Ask My Mother Her Favorite Color"

Exit 13: "Early Morning Flight"

Lips: "At the Tenement Museum," "Calamity"

On the Verge: Poetry of the Palisades III (NJLC): "Windthrow"

Paterson Literary Review: "An Old Invention," "After the Junior High Sadie Hawkins Dance," "A Secret Correspondence," "What I Can't Explain," "Wonderland"

The Constellation of Kisses: "Like Koi in Deep Water"

The Corner NPPC: "During the Pandemic"

The Practicing Poet: "Tennis Player's Lament"

The Stillwater Review: "Talking to God," "My Great Mistake"

The Strategic Poet: Honing the Craft: "Dreaming the Garden State," "The Whole Earth is like a Poem"

Tiferet: "Where the Soul Speaks Out in Conversation"

US 1 Worksheets: "Dining Alfresco"

"Golden Bell," "The Main Thing," "Maple Tree" are anthologized in *Offerings: Tiferet Spiritual Chapbook vol. I.* "Library Visitor" is anthologized in *Moonstone Poetry Series*

Featured Poetry Anthology. "Everything, Everywhere," "Pure Mathematics," and "What's in a Kiss" are anthologized in the *Wanaque Academic Center Adult Anthology.*

Notes

"A Secret Correspondence" received Editor's Choice in the Allen Ginsberg Poetry Awards, 2018.

"The Whole Earth Is like a Poem," title drawn from "The Sun" by Czeslaw Milosz.

"Where the Soul Speaks Out in Conversation" was one of ten finalists in the Tiferet poetry contest, 2021. Inspiration for the poem was a quote from Walt Whitman, "I loaf and invite my soul."

CPSIA information can be obtained
at www.ICGtesting.com
Printed in the USA
JSHW050527260722
28534JS00005B/18